Zen Bride™

by Nora Cabrera

RUNNING PRESS
PHILADELPHIA · LONDON

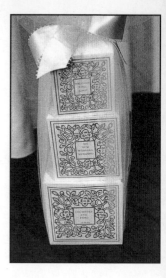

9 8 7 6 5 4 3 2 1
Digit on the right indicates the number of this printing.

Library of Congress Cataloging-in-Publication Number
2005922020

ISBN 0-7624-2435-4

Designed by Gwen Galeone
Edited by Lindsay Powers

This kit may be ordered by mail from the publisher.
Please include $2.50 for postage and handling.
But try your bookstore first!

Running Press Book Publishers
125 South Twenty-second Street
Philadelphia, Pennsylvania 19103-4399

Visit us on the web!
www.runningpress.com

Contents

Welcome
Zen Bride

"Live the life you've dreamed."

—HENRY DAVID THOREAU

THE BEGINNING

Congratulations! You must be reading this book right now because you're happily engaged and excitedly planning your wedding. This is probably one of the most exciting times in your life (hooray)! And most stressful (boo-hiss).

I too was once newly engaged and planning my wedding. Ahh, how I long for those blissful days... *yeah right!* I had seen countless friends go down the "bridezilla" road, driven mad by the wedding planning stress, details, and potential mishaps—not to mention the family induced dramas. When it came my time, I promised myself that I would be different—that I would not succumb to the stress of it all, I would not become that dreaded bridezilla.

I had spent the prior two years studying and practicing Feng Shui, and working hard to bring balance into my own life and the lives of others. Yoga, meditation, and eating healthy were all a part of my daily routine. Trust me, the routine was never perfect—I had my off moments but they weren't the norm. When the serious wedding planning began, I promised myself that I would not stress while I planned—I would overcome! Sound familiar? Read on my friends, read on . . .

Alas, soon after my well-intentioned promise, the stress and amount of work completely overtook me. I WAS FREAKING OUT! As I immersed myself in the planning process, with more and more details and endless decisions to make (*did I really want lemon filling or would my marriage be guaranteed to last if I went for the raspberry filling?*) I saw how easy it was to lose sight of the meaning of "matrimony."

THE MEANING OF MATRIMONY

Let's pause here and look up the word matrimony and its meaning according to Webster:

Main Entry: mat·ri·mo·ny

Pronunciation: 'ma-tr&-"mO-nE

Function: *noun*: the union of man and woman as husband and wife: MARRIAGE

Oh right—I knew that. Of course it was about committing myself to the man (the right man!) I wanted to spend the rest of my life with day after day. And that's exactly what I was focusing on—not! Most of the time I was focused on the details of how my wedding would look on the outside. Not that there is anything wrong with that—it is quite necessary. But the problem was that there was no *balance:* all outside, no inside. There was very little attention focused on how *I* was feeling inside, and how *I* would and should feel on the actual day of the wedding. Everything everyone said about the unavoidable stress of wedding planning was absolutely coming true. I was not happy about this, but resigned myself to believing *"this is just the way it is when a bride plans her wedding."*

One day, in the throws of "planning" turmoil, I found myself driving and popping in a relaxing music tape. I was desperately attempting to find some peace (or at least a space in which to find some) in the midst of the chaos. I began to ponder and contemplate, quite a rare occurrence during these times, on how I was proceeding through all this madness. And I realized that in fact, I *had* become that totally stressed out bride! *The horror.*

At that moment I thought, "There's got to be a better way." And that's when I decided all brides need a little coaching to help them remember themselves through the chaos of wedding planning.

That's exactly what this book and lavender products are here to do. It's all about giving yourself permission to find time and space to relax. And having some delicious spa products to indulge in can't hurt!

If at times you falter, and you will falter, take a minute (or two, as many as you need!) and focus on one of the serene black and white photographs in this book and / or read one of the many positive affirmation quotes. Please, take some time for yourself during these trying times and remember to enjoy your journey of wedding planning. It's a journey meant to get you to your destination:

marrying the love of your life.

Sage Advice

"Remember that happiness is a way
of travel, not a destination."

—ROY GOODMAN

S o now we're completely clear that your wedding day is one of the most important days of your entire life and we're also clear on the fact that planning your wedding is one of the most stressful experiences of your entire life.

Remember that your wedding is about celebrating the fact that you are marrying the *one*:

• the one who makes your heart go pitter-patter

• the one in a billion

• the one (the only) one who will offer to rub your feet

   (can I get his number. . .)

• the one who loves you right now and simply smiles when you

   go off the deep end because of some small wedding detail like

   the daisies are supposed to have 7 petals each, not 6!

   (Yes, I know NO detail is small right now.)

For that's the *One* you're going to spend the rest of your life with—the one you will weather life's unexpected moments, those joyful moments, those sorrowful moments, those angry moments, those funny moments, and all the other moments in between. Try to think of this wedding planning time as your dress rehearsal for life—a glimpse into how to take on all the expected and anticipated moments as well as those completely unexpected moments.

"Marriage—as its veterans know well—is the continuous process of getting used to things you hadn't expected."

—Tom Mullen

This is the time to really take care of yourself and that's the hardest part right now. It's almost like I'm asking you to keep your feet on the ground while a Category 5 Hurricane is blowing around you. But this really is the time to stay grounded and be ever present.

How do you do this? Well, keep reading! I'm going to do my best to help you. We'll find your balance by visiting all the important areas of your being: mind, body, spirit and heart. The point is to be present and to live, to experience your wedding day—not go through it like a deer in headlights! Trust me, you can do this. It is easier said than done, but you can.

Be Content From the Inside Out

> "I have noticed that folks are generally about as happy as they make up their minds to be."
>
> —Abraham Lincoln

*H*ow wonderful that you have found your way to your own Zen Bride relaxation kit! There are so many ways to help you maintain your Zen Bride center while planning your wedding; lots of ideas spread throughout this book. But we also know that many days you don't want to read or do anymore—you just want to *be!* Some delicious items have been included in your kit to do just that—help you "be" a Zen Bride!

All of the products included in Zen Bride have one thing in common—lavender! Lavender helps one experience natural relaxation and inspiring calm . . . so you can see how it is very fitting to help the bride become a Zen Bride.

A little Lavender 101, if you will. Native to the Mediterranean, lavender is now grown all over the world. True lavender is an evergreen, woody shrub that has violet-blue flowering tops. It has been used for fragrant baths and to enhance a variety of body care products. Its name is derived from the Latin word "lavare," meaning to wash or to bathe. It has since become known as a very powerful remedy and has a variety of uses. Feeling relaxed already? Read on, there's more.

One of the most unique characteristics of lavender is that it is not just for energizing or relaxing, but also for balancing. The scent of lavender will rejuvenate and inspire a tired soul and relax, soothe and slow down someone who is stressed or tense (yes, this means you)! We can harness the power of lavender to add balance and serenity to our increasingly hectic lives (translation: a bride in the throws of wedding planning). Lavender is able to reestablish a person's balanced, harmonious, and natural state, without the use of synthetic chemicals. It is the all-natural remedy. So simple, so zen, so perfect for you, stressed-out bride.

Here are some quick ideas to help you dive into Zen Bride bliss (calm and peace):

Lavender Hints:

1. Adding lavender to your bath helps you relax and reduce tension.

2. Inhaling the soothing scent of lavender throughout the day can help alleviate stress and tension.

3. Lavender has been proven to have a positive influence on depression and irritability.

4. For a good night's sleep, put some lavender next to your bed. Studies have proven lavender's effectiveness as a relaxation aid, along with its safety. A drop or two is all you need!

The Zen Bride lavender products are fairly self-explanatory, but here are a few suggestions for use:

BATH SALTS

These luxurious lavender bath salts are the perfect excuse to close the world out, draw a bath, and soak up all the positive benefits of taking some quality, quiet time for yourself.

Hint: When it's hard to tune out the overactive brain, or seems down right impossible, sometimes a little relaxing music is just what you need to help those bath salts unwind you!

AROMATHERAPY CANDLE

So now you've got the warm bath with lavender salts and perhaps some nice music but you're still having a hard time trying to unwind? Hmmmmmm, could it be that your bathroom lights are on full blast? This would be a perfect time to light your lavender aromatherapy candle to help create a little mood lighting!

Hint: There are other mood lighting situations in which your Zen Bride lavender candle would be great as well . . .

SILKY SLEEP MASK

Sometimes we all just need to close our eyes and get away from it all, easier said than done right?! So whether it is in the bathtub soaking in soothing lavender suds or in bed, use the sleep mask to help you escape. It's portable, convenient, and travels well—so take it with you and use anytime, anywhere and tune in to *you*!

Hint: Sleep masks and aromatherapy scents (like lavender) work wonders together!

Notice the pink lotus flower on the sleep mask. Lotus flowers are beautiful and powerfully symbolic:

The pink lotus is the supreme lotus, generally reserved for the highest deity. The Lotus flower has for thousands of years symbolized spiritual enlightenment. Indeed, this flower essence's purpose is to accelerate spiritual evolvement and enhance healing on every level within the system.

Lotuses of many colors grow in Asia, Egypt, the Americas, and Australia, and in all these places it has been used as a symbol. Theosophy interprets this symbolism as alluding to the unfoldment of the inner divine potential, and two parallels between spiritual and physical planes and between cosmic creation and spiritual rebirth. Moreover, because it has buds, blossoms, and seed pods simultaneously on the same plant, it has symbolized the past, present, and future. How very Zen!

ROOM MIST

Three words: instant stress relief! Lavender room mist is the perfect way to instantly lift your spirits and let go of the heavy load. Just a spritz or two and voilà!

Hint: Spray this lightly on your linens to help lull you into peaceful slumber.

All it takes is a few minutes of permission to let go and allow the stress to fall away—and you've got words of wisdom and these lovely Zen Bride lavender goodies to help you! A few minutes now will be so worth it when you look back on how you spent this last year, planning your wedding. And more importantly, how you arrive at your wedding day is just important as the wedding day itself! Inhale ZEN, Exhale BRIDE!

DO I SMELL LAVENDER ALREADY?

Mind

**"Two souls but a single thought.
Two hearts that beat as one."**

—STACEY Q.

*A*s soon as you were engaged, I'm sure your mind began to drift, imagining all the wonderful things that you'd want for your wedding. As the celebration of your engagement winds down and the reality of planning sets in—those blissful thoughts have now all turned into a million and one stressful details (ok—I know some brides out there will have over *2 million* details they're stressing over). Suddenly, you find your mind crowded with so many decisions to make and so much to do that you feel like your brain is going to explode. This feeling is a true sign that you *are* planning your wedding. Nobody needs to pinch you now, you know you're not dreaming!

I could lie to you at this point and say that it will get easier once you make all your big decisions but the truth of the matter is: the details will not go away (they actually get more intense) and you will probably carry them with you all the way up until your wedding day. Makes you want to put down the book right now and elope, right? Wait a second, take a deep breath and then release it, breathe, please breathe!

Though eloping seems to be an appealing option for a whole slew of reasons (mainly, preserving your sanity), most brides decide to hunker down, dig deep, and take the plunge. The challenge then is how to manage those details and decisions without compromising all of your sanity and checking yourself into an asylum! Below are six Zen Bride suggestions to help keep your *mind* (after all, I doubt your fiancé wants to marry the woman of his dreams without her mind!):

1. Create a beautiful wedding space.

With so many details, it's hard to focus on the bigger (more important) picture. Designate a space—a shelf or a table—where you can create a small area dedicated to the man and wedding of your dreams. You can put anything in this space as long as you follow the Zen Bride golden rule: it has to make you FEEL good if you look at it.

The idea with this space is to give you a place that's already made that instantly makes you feel great about the man you are going to marry and the wedding you are planning. Sometimes when we are so stressed out, it's almost impossible to switch off the stress and anxiety and move into "joy" mode. By creating this space, the work will have already been done and your beautiful space will be waiting when you need a quick dose of "perfect wedding / happily ever after!"

2. Take time out to do something you enjoy that is not wedding related at least once a week.

What I mean by this is that you have to rest your brain! Most creative people will confess that their greatest inspiration comes when they're not thinking, much less stressing or worrying. As much as you can justify that by working on the wedding you are doing something for you, it's not the same. You have to learn to take care of yourself first (ladies pay attention here!). If you are so stressed and spent from a year of wedding planning when you reach your wedding day, I can guarantee you that you will not be able to enjoy marrying the man of your dreams. An image that comes to mind to illustrate my point: *have you ever seen a totally stressed out ballet dancer dance?* No! You see grace, and ease, and effortlessness, you see someone who is fully in the moment of loving to dance! And so should a bride on her wedding day be graceful, and grounded, and happy, not stressed, not carrying the last year of planning on her shoulders—you get my point, yes?

So please, get out once a week and do something for you, the woman: yoga, dinner with friends (only if you forbid wedding talk), pottery class—you get the picture! I promise that the great feelings and inspiration from giving this kind of time to yourself will spill out into your wedding planning.

3. Create a wedding "to do" time line.

This should be one of the first things you do. Because before you do anything else—lesson number 1 is that you can't do it all at once—and there is soooooooooo much to do. So by creating this timeline, you will better (and with less stress) be able to prioritize what needs to get done when.

Look for hints in wedding magazines and on wedding internet sites. Talk to other women you know who have been down this road—get the real scoop on realistic deadlines. However, don't let all the traditional "checklists" get to you, as they have a tendency to be rather daunting. Put things in perspective and be realistic about what needs to get accomplished, and when.

4. Decide what is most important in your planning.

There will be many, many, many, many (ok—many times infinity) choices that you are going to have to make and along with that comes compromise. If you know ahead of time what can be flexible and what needs to absolutely be set in stone and the things that will fall in between . . . you will be SOOOO ahead of the game. This way you know what you are going to expend your energy on and to what degree.

5. Positive thoughts create a positive reality.

Think positive (what I really mean here is FEEL positive). Yes, there are going to be people, things, and more that might stress you out and in those moments you are not going to be feeling great, that's just the reality. BUT, how long you decide "not to feel great" is up to you. It will be a much more enjoyable journey if you decide you are going to always choose now "to make the best of it." Go through the tough times while always keeping your focus on the good times and more importantly focus on whom you love and what the planning is all about!

6. Organize your thoughts and the one million things you want for your wedding . . . Use the Journal section designated at the back of this book to help you get organized. Most brides also have some sort of binder to keep all things wedding in.
There are always going to be a million things you feel you have to handle, decide, plan, etc. when it comes to your wedding. That you have to do all this is a moot point—but how you do it can be negotiated. I hope these suggestions help give you the opportunity to be a bit more zen in your planning:

grace under pressure is always divine!

THE BRIDE AS PSYCHIC?

Now, another big job you probably have while planning your wedding is that of WEDDING PSYCHIC. What I mean is: not only are you expected to handle the million details—you're also supposed to "foresee" what *might* go wrong and then plan for it not to . . . am I right? So here you are, happy as can be because you're marrying the man of your dreams and yet you're totally stressed out because you're trying to stop things from going wrong before they've even happened! It's understandable that this comes with the job but how helpful is it for you to be thinking 24/7 about what might go WRONG with your wedding? Between the stress and the problem solving, there's not that much room left for joy and positive thinking to find you. And that's the key, *you* have to make the effort to think positively!

That's why we're going to take a moment right now (this includes you!) and put together some positive thoughts and feelings so that you have a "positive / joy" bag to grab from when you're at your wits end (yes I know—you're there already . . .) Have a friend do the writing so you can focus on the "positive vibing" here. Divide a piece of paper into 3 columns:

1. In the first column, list your top five wedding/what could go wrong fears.

For example: My biggest fear is that is will be pouring rain on my wedding day.

2. Now, take a moment to visualize how you would handle or solve this problem if it was to happen (positive outcomes only please!). See yourself solving this problem easily, with grace, and most importantly: see (feel!) yourself happy with the outcome of how you were able to solve this problem.

For example: It's pouring rain on my wedding day and the "Plan B" I created goes into motion and everyone knows what to do already, including the caterer, photographer, and my bridesmaids! I see things unfolding smoothly and everything happening as it should—especially the fact that I'm marrying the man of my dreams!

3. After each visualization write down briefly how you handled this problem in the 2nd column.

4. Now finally, in the 3rd column write down a positive statement after having turned your negative fear into a positive.

For example: Everything is going smoothly on my wedding day, rain or shine—and everyone knows what to do!

Top 5 Wedding Day Fears (What Could Go Wrong)	How To Handle The Problem	Positive Statement
1. It's raining! (not men)	I have a Plan B!	*I'm marrying the man of my dreams.*
2. Red wine on wedding dress!	I have a back-up dress.	*I will feel beautiful inside and out.*
3. Bouquet is ugly!	I can use bridesmaids flowers.	*I'm creative and flexible.*
4. Officiant is late!	I have contact information.	*He/she will get here.*
5. Goes by too fast!	Breathe, relax, and enjoy.	*I will be present for what is important.*

5. Now, flip to the Journal section at the back of this book and make a list of all your final positive statements. Carry the Zen Bride book (that conveniently doubles as a journal) around with you at all times for quick and easy reference.

Any time you find yourself getting overwhelmed worrying about the things you can't foresee or control (like the weather), take a moment to find and focus on a thought that feels better. Wouldn't you rather think happy thoughts about your wedding anyway? Have a look at one of the black and white images in this book, they are sure to evoke positive sentiments and an overall feeling of inner calm. Go ahead, smile! Did you know it takes more muscles to frown than to smile? It's true!

SMILE!

Body

"To love and be loved is to feel
the sun from both sides."

—David Viscott

*W*ell, now that we've touched on your MIND and the wedding, let's take a moment to focus on BODY. Ladies, it's all about balance during this time!

Brides report all kinds of different ways they begin to feel the stress of the wedding. There are tense shoulders, headaches, queasy stomachs, and insomnia—just to name a few. And usually the body stress corresponds to the mental stress, right? That kink in your neck: getting your invitations out on time; the constant dull headache, seating table issues . . . I'm sure you already know (and feel!) what your body / stress issues are already! Serenity Now!

So then the question is "do you do anything about it and if so, then what?" The secret isn't so much what you choose to do—but that you make a CHOICE (and stick with it) to do something to alleviate the stress! Again, we will revisit one of the suggestions in the previous chapter: do something to get your mind—and BODY off the wedding. Not everyone chooses bungee jumping and that's OK. The secret is to do something physical—even if its just some stretching exercises at the end of the day. Just because you get into bed at the end of a long day and will away your stress—does not mean that your body will get the message. You have to do *something* to loosen up and expel the physical tension your body is holding. Most people think that just by going to bed—when you rest your mind—that your body will unwind and relax on its own . . . sooooooooooo not true! Your body will wake up with the same tension it went to bed with the night before. And so you wake up in the morning and that knot in your upper right shoulder is still there and you're trying to rub it out and voilà! You remember that the knot is probably there for wedding stress detail #37 and well, now you better go deal with that detail—and what has just happened? The tension in your body has just snapped your (rested) mind back into stress mode! Even if it is only five minutes of gentle stretching in bed before you go to sleep—do it!

Now I know the million things you have on your plate so I've made a list of some simple yoga relaxation stretches that will make your body feel yummy and your mind will thank me since that's one less thing you have to figure out!

FIVE SIMPLE ZEN BRIDE STRESS RELEASE EXERCISES

1. Splendid Neck Stretch

2. Sublime Shoulder Shrugs

3. Heavenly Ear Tug Massage

4. Blissful Back Rolls

5. Peaceful Child's Pose

Note: For each of these exercises, please make sure that all inhalations and exhalations are long, deep, and ALWAYS through your nose. By breathing through your mouth, you evoke the flight or fight (stress) response from your body.

1. Splendid Neck Stretch

Sit comfortably with your back and neck straight. Begin moving your head slowly to the right as if you are trying to touch your ear to your shoulder. Move very slowly, noticing tension (especially your shoulders tightening up!) and breathing through the stretch. Switch sides, now moving your head to the left. Next, slowly move your head forward, trying to touch your chin to your chest. Let the weight of your head deepen the stretch once your chin is resting on your chest. Also take note if you're clenching your jaw during this exercise—release, release (breathe) and release!

2. Sublime Shoulder Shrugs

Again, sit comfortably with your back and neck straight. As you inhale, lift your shoulders straight up as if you are trying to touch your ears with them. Exhale as you drop your shoulders down. Repeat this "up / down" movement for at least 12 cycles. When you are done and your shoulders are down, take one final deep breath to release the tension.

3. Heavenly Ear Tug Massage

Take your index finger and thumb and slowly massage the edges of your ears. Also gently tug on your ears as you are doing this massage. This is a great one to offer to do on your love—a quick way to get him to fall in love with you all over again!

4. Blissful Back Rolls

Lie on your back and with your arms, hug your knees to your chest. Rock back and forth in this position at least six times. Rock with a steady motion but not too fast.

5. Peaceful Child's Pose

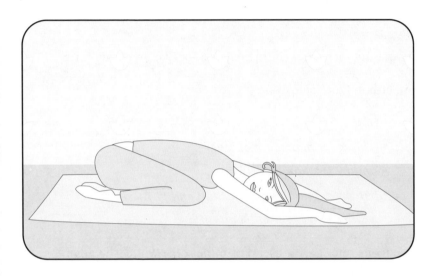

Sit on the floor with your buttocks resting on your calves. Bend your body forward with your arms extended until your hands, arms, and face touch the floor. Hold this pose for at least 3 minutes, taking slow deep breaths in and out through the nose, making a point to release the tension on the exhale breath.

Your body and mind will thank you for these stretches and moments to let go and just be!

Zen Mind + Zen Body = Zen Bride!

Preparing for your wedding day is a lot like preparing for a marathon. You have to be:

- *in shape for endurance*
- *relaxed for maximum output*
- *healthy for stamina*
- *rested for quick reflexes (mental and physical)*
- *positive to make it to the finish line*

Someone once gave a friend of mine some wonderful advice before running a marathon, which can also be applied to all the events surrounding and leading up to your wedding day. Make sure to take a moment to really look around and take it all in, else before you know it, it's going to be over. Take some mental snapshots and engrave them into your memory. Don't forget to smile. Be grateful for all the details, big and small, and recognize that you are surrounded by people you love, who are cheering you on, each and every step of the way.

THE BOBE

Another common occurrence with brides is something I like to call the BOBE which stands for Bride's Out of Body Experience. And it does not happen only on the wedding day. Perhaps you have witnessed it with other brides: the glazed look, the total freak out, the wanting to run far, far away look.

The reason I mention it is because when you can recognize that it's happening to you—it's *really* time to take a break. It's almost like when you have too many appliances going on at the same time in your home and all of a sudden everything shuts off. This is a sign that it's time to unplug—even if just for half an hour.

Please listen to your body and what it is trying to tell you— I promise you will be a happier bride—and a more relaxed one as well!

...relax

Spirit and Heart

"Now join your hands, and with your hands your hearts."

—WILLIAM SHAKESPEARE

S o, we've gone over mental stress, and body stress but there's also what I like to call "perfect wedding stress syndrome." Chances are that you have already bought the obligatory 15+ wedding magazines and flipped through all the pictures and ads and you may have already seen a wedding show or two—maybe on Celebrity Weddings? Perfect weddings, perfect million dollar budget, perfect dress, perfect weather, perfect table setting and the list goes on . . .

Whether you have $10 to spend on your wedding or $1,000,000—it's not about doing it all. It's about doing what you can do—making it personal, making it special to you. I guarantee that the people who come to your wedding will not remember the 1,000 details that are exactly like the other 20 weddings they've been to in their lives. They will remember the details of the wedding that are personal to you and your fiancé—the special details that are you.

Sometimes with so many details on your mind and the added stress of all decisions (big and small) needing to be perfect—it's hard to hear what your heart is telling you. Here's a fun, quick, and simple exercise to help get to the heart of your wedding.

THE DESERT ISLAND EXERCISE:

Sit down with your fiancé, each with a piece of paper and pencil. Suspend all logical reasoning.

You know you're going to be stranded on a desert island with your fiancé. But this is no ordinary island—it is full of everything you need in terms of necessities for now and into the future—shelter, food, bed, etc. There is even a way to access any information you might need (like how to build a boat, help a woman give birth—you get the point). But obviously, there is *nothing* personal in the space or on the island. You both are allowed to bring 5 items—and they can be anything. What are the 10 things you and your fiancé would choose to bring?

I will give you short example of a current couple who are getting married in a few months. Let's peek at their lists:

HER List:

1. Music that we both love that makes us laugh, smile, and cry.
2. Pictures of family and friends close to our hearts.
3. My stuffed animal that I've had since birth, Belle.
4. Todd would bring his surfboard, because surfing is his passion.
5. I'd bring journals so I can write, because writing is my passion.

HIS List:

1. Photo album of all our family and friends.

2. Surfboard.

3. Swiss army knife my grandmother gave me from her travels.

4. Journal that Lindsay gave me before I went off to Europe.

5. Case of our favorite wine & spirits (Rum? Coronas with Lime)

Now from their lists, this is what I would tell them:

First, drink the rum now, while you plan the wedding. Just kidding (sort of). Ok, seriously, this is what I would say to them:

Your lists show you the important elements you should have at your wedding. You don't have to choose everything from the list but for instance—the importance of surfboards and journals— perhaps that could be the unique favor for your guests—a journal with a surfboard print. Pictures of friends and family seems to be very important also—why not have a table set up with your most important pictures or incorporate them into your reception tables—that would make a very personal touch.

Once you're done with your list, take another look at what you've written. Chances are—there are some things in the list that you would like to incorporate into your wedding (if you haven't done so already)! These items don't have to be incorporated literally either—they can find a way into your wedding symbolically.

The possibilities could be endless, depending on what you've written down on your desert island list! What makes this exercise important is that it helps you bypass your "logical/rational" brain (which always seems to be on overdrive during wedding planning) and helps you go directly to the "heart" (your heart) of what might be important to have at your wedding. Your lists might reveal things you hadn't even thought of yet!

So when you find yourself overwhelmed because you don't know what the right choice would be to make your "perfect" wedding—make the choice that makes YOU happiest—something that makes you smile—let your feelings be your guide. The personal, unique touches that you add will, in the end make your wedding special and memorable.

Choose with your heart and you will be happiest. What makes a wedding perfect is the way everyone feels—bring on the love and the joy!

The Scents
of Serenity

**"To love deeply in one direction makes
us more loving in all others."**

—ANNE SOPHIE SWETCHINE

*O*k, so you've got the mental and physical exercises to help you relax and zen out . . . but what happens when you're at your wits end and have no time or patience to really take a time out to "do" anything? This is where aromatherapy comes to the rescue!

In case you're new to this, aromatherapy can be loosely defined as the use of essential oils to promote health and well being. What are essential oils you may ask? Highly concentrated oils derived from flowers, fruit, roots, and bark of plants.

You probably see the word aromatherapy attached to almost all and any product that is for body or home. But, it's important to know that not all smells are alike. And just because something smells good doesn't mean that it's actually working to promote your health and well-being. Be sure to buy essential oils that are rated as "therapeutic grade." Also, no matter how great you read an oil might be for your particular situation—smell first. No sense in forcing yourself to smell something you don't like—the nose knows! Remember, a drop or two is all you need.

Here are some of the most helpful essential oils and their emotional healing benefits for a Zen Bride:

BERGAMOT

A sweet oil that brings about balance, chases away depression and helplessness, and encourages relaxation and feelings of joy.

CHAMOMILE ROMAN

Encourages calmness and emotional stability, promotes relaxation (and cooperation when needed!)

EUCALYPTUS

This oil will not only clear your nose but your mind as well! Increases concentration and helps with rationality. A great oil to inhale when you have a cold due to its antibacterial properties.

GERANIUM

Use this lovely oil to bring your emotions into balance and to uplift them. This is also a great oil when you need to feel supported (female / mother energy). Do not use during pregnancy.

GRAPEFRUIT

Feeling depressed and disconnected? This oil is for you! Encourages positive thinking, confidence, and joy. This is a great oil when you need to reconnect—mind, body, and spirit.

JASMINE

Reach for this one to stop negative thinking (fear and nervous tension also) in its tracks. Encourages optimism and harmony. A great oil when you need a little inspiration.

LAVENDER

What wouldn't you use this oil for? Helps with insomnia, relieves stress, balances emotions, encourages gentleness and acceptance. Ever had that "I can't breathe!" feeling? This is the oil to help you *breathe.* A great breathing, reenergizing, stress relieving blend: one part lavender and one part eucalyptus. Reminder: All of the products in this kit have lavender in them!

ORANGE

Orange you glad to see me? (Oh come on, laugh!) When you find yourself obsessing about the wedding details—let go with orange! You get sunlight and happiness in one whiff. This one promotes lightheartedness, creativity, and positive thinking. Total joy in a drop.

PEPPERMINT

Focus power! Say goodbye to mental blocks. A great oil for increasing concentration and reenergizing old tired thoughts. Do not use during pregnancy.

SANDALWOOD

This beautiful oil brings you back in touch with your own inner wisdom and at the same time helps you feel grounded. It's like reaching for the heavens without fear, knowing your feet are on the ground. Promotes warmth and serenity. Encourages harmony, peace, and insightfulness.

Believe it or not, your sense of smell is about 10,000 times more sensitive than any of your other senses. That makes using aromatherapy quite a powerful option in helping you relax! There are many ways that aromatherapy can be incorporated into your Zen Bride relaxation regimen. Therapeutic grade essential oils are best to use when you're talking about aromatherapy and they are highly concentrated—so ALWAYS go easy! Too much of an oil may cause the opposite effects. **For example:** Too much lavender will end up stimulating you instead of helping you relax or sleep.

Here are a few examples for use:

Blissful Bath

Put 5-6 drops of essential oils in a nice warm bath and soak for at least 20 minutes. Be sure to add the oils *after* you're done adding the bath water. Adding the oils at the beginning of running your bath water only means that they will be evaporated by the time you get in.

Helpful hint: put a little milk (yes milk!) in your bath water to help your oils last longer and soften your skin.

Drop on the Go

Need help ASAP? Use one (no more than 2, as essential oils are extremely concentrated) drop(s) and apply to wrists, behind the ears, ear lobes, etc. Once you're done—take a moment to bring your hands to your nose and take three deep inhalations through your nose—inhaling all the positive benefits of the oil you're using.

Misting Magic

Change your stagnant surroundings instantly. Ever feel like you've hit a wall because you can feel them all around you in your space? If yes, then this is the way to go. Fill an empty spray bottle with 4-8 oz. spring or distilled water, add about 10 drops of your essential oil of choice and give a few quick spritzes—you'll instantly feel better wherever you are!

Helpful hint: The lavender room mist included in this kit works well for this purpose.

With so much to think about, decide on, and do with planning your wedding—aromatherapy is a perfect Zen Bride solution. Keep these oils in mind for your wedding day too. Happiness and calmness can be found in the scents of serenity.

Zen Ways to
Fast Relaxation

"Elope from the wedding planning so that you may be present for the wedding."

—Nora Cabrera

Quick suggestions that will help you relax NOW!

1. Boogie down! Turn on your music and dance, dance, dance. People may look at you funny, just ignore them; it's a great way to unwind.

2. If you need to yell, yell into a pillow—take your frustrations out on it, not anyone else!

3. Do something nice for someone. This should lift your spirits and make you feel good about yourself.

4. Exercise! Get that heart pumpin' and start releasing endorphins! Sex is also good for this.

5. Get outside! Expose yourself to natural light and breathe in the fresh air. Build a snowman, plant in the garden or bbq your favorite foods. This will help energize you.

6. Get your zzz's! Sleep can help improve mood, energy, and concentration.

7. Take your vitamins! Make sure you are getting all the proper nutrients through food and vitamins. A healthy bride is a beautiful bride and plus, there's a no fainting policy on your own wedding day!

8. Have a pajama party and relax with the girls. Remember when life was "simple?" When we were young and didn't have a care in the world? Take yourself back to that time in your life and relive it again as an adult. Smiles came easy then, and they should now too! Remember this on your wedding day and flash your pearly whites for all to see.

9. Be content. Be happy with what you can afford and philosophical about how things turn out. Focus on what you have and be grateful.

10. Laugh often—there is humor in everything, find it!

One to grow on—Breathe. Close your eyes, free your mind and breathe in and out through your nose. A few simple long, deep breaths will help you reduce tension and stress, and regain clarity and balance.

DO NOT DISTURB

Face Your
Fears
Meditation

"The great secret of a successful marriage
is to treat all disasters as incidents and
none of the incidents as disasters."

—HAROLD NICOLSON

*W*hat we always seem to fear the most is the unknown. And when it's your wedding— that fear is about not knowing what might go wrong. For that reason, I find it helpful to take a few minutes to do this meditation so that when you are faced with those unknown moments on your wedding day—you will already know how to handle them—at least emotionally. So dig deep, find your biggest wedding day fear, and dive in!

P.S. I suggest doing this meditation only once and that you do it with only one fear—not all of them! The point of this is not to keep rehashing your fears. It's about acknowledging them so you can then let them go.

Find a quiet place with no distractions to do this. This would also be a great time to use a little aromatherapy. Pick an oil that you feel would be helpful to you during this meditation. Mist your room (you could use the lavender room mist included in this kit) or apply a drop of one of your favorite soothing oils to your wrist before you begin, or light the lavender candle.

Enlist the help of a trusted friend or even your fiancé to read aloud this meditation to you or pre-record and then play back the meditation when you are ready:

Note: Take a moment to settle in and get comfortable. Look around and make sure that there will be no outer distractions for the next few minutes. When you are ready, close your eyes.

I want you to take three deep breaths. Slowly inhale and exhale through your nose. Breathe in and out. Breathe in and out and one last time, breathe in and out.

Now, imagine yourself walking down a long corridor. You notice that this corridor is glowing with pale green and pink light. As you are walking, you see a door at the end of the corridor. As you approach this door, you realize that when you open the door, you will see your biggest wedding day fear coming true. You are now at the door. Take a deep breath here . . . Wiggle your toes and feel your feet on the ground. When you are ready, open the door and walk in. Take a few moments to see what is going on. What wedding day fear are you seeing before your eyes? Take another deep breath. Now take a moment to find a mirror. You can now see yourself—notice how beautiful and calm you look. Look into your eyes and know that whatever the problem is—you can handle it. You now see your new husband and he looks so happy. You see the love and the joy in his eyes. You know that together you can handle anything. See all the other people at the wedding: family, friends—everyone there. You see in their faces that they are happy and having a wonderful time, they are celebrating your marriage. You look around your wedding one last time and see that your biggest fear is completely gone. All you see and feel now is excitement, joy, and love. When you are ready, start to walk to the door. Take a deep breath as you take one last look at your beautiful wedding. You are now back in the corridor closing the door. As you walk back in the glow of the pale green and pink light, you are smiling because you know that no matter what happens—it will be taken care of and you will be fine. You smile with the feeling of seeing so much love and joy and merriment at your wedding. You are now back in your room. When you are ready, slowly open your eyes.

See? That wasn't so bad! Don't you feel great now?! It's quite wonderful to know that you can handle anything that might (or might not) come at you on your wedding day. And from now on—focus on the positive—see and focus on all the beautiful things that are going to happen!

My editor's father once gave her a valuable piece of advice, which directly correlates to just about anything in life: "Set your expectation level to a realistic point so you will never be disappointed."

Final Poetic Advice

"Let us celebrate the occasion with wine and sweet words."

—Plautus

So, you wake up on your wedding day and breathe a sigh of relief because well A. you've made it this far, B. everything is set and has agreed to go perfectly, C. you're going to marry the love of your life. Fabulous, right? Yes—especially regarding letter C!

And maybe for letters A. and B. "Maybe?" you ask, "why maybe?" Because it all depends on you. Your wedding day is like a dress rehearsal for the rest of your life. As much planning as you've done for the past year of your life—there are always going to be variables—things outside your control.

You can't choose what will go smoothly and what won't on your wedding day but you can choose how you're going to handle the little surprises that might come your way that day. And more importantly, you get to choose what you focus your feelings on. Will you be feeling the love for your love or will you be feeling anger because the florist sent daisies instead of orchids? Get out of your head—all the thoughts and details of how you've planned the wedding—and live the beautiful moments that will be right in front of you.

Decide before your wedding day that you are going to make the best of it—no matter what "it" is. Let go of all the wedding planning and control so that you may be present for the real event—your ceremony of marriage.

A few helpful hints:

1. Exchange love letters with your fiancé the night before the wedding. A great way to disconnect from all the stress of the wedding preparations and to connect with your love!

2. Book a massage the morning of your wedding. No matter how "prepared" you think you are—it's hard to stay grounded with such an exciting day ahead of you. A massage is a perfect way to help you relax, let go of stress, and get grounded right down to your core.

3. Eat light and strong meals for breakfast and lunch. Pick things that are high in protein and light on the carbs. You want to feel satisfied—not full! Make sure you drink plenty of water and stay away from caffeine, which will only increase your jitters and make you dehydrated!

4. Designate a girlfriend to be the lipstick police. Your make-up should last through the ceremony and reception but your lipstick will probably need to be reapplied more often so you look perfect for all those wedding pictures. Make sure someone is there to remind you of when it's time to reapply so you don't have to keep checking!

5. Peek in on your reception site completely set up before the guests go in. Once you enter your reception it will be a constant whirlwind of people, food, music, dancing, and celebration, all great things. But having taken a private moment to see your reception site completely set up, will be a wonderful personal moment for you and your new husband.

As important as a wedding is to a bride, if you boil it down to its essence—it's just a party (usually a 3 to 4 hour one) to celebrate the real event—marriage (a sacred union for the rest of your life) to the one you love. A Zen Bride once suggested:

love

YOUR NEW HUSBAND, & ENJOY THE PARTY!

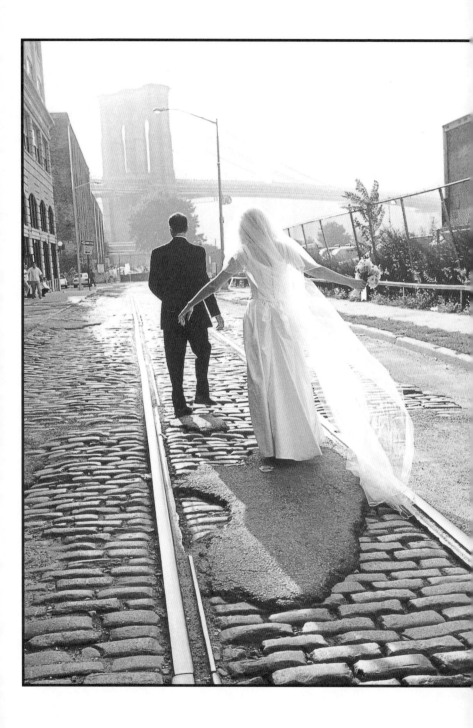

Happily
Ever After

"With you I will walk my path from this day forward."

—WEDDING VOW

S o you're married—now what?! Stop! If you are attempting to read this chapter before you've gotten married—stop now! This chapter is not for you! You have enough to do and think about! Seriously people, step away from this chapter.

If you're opening up to read this chapter back from your honeymoon with that newlywed glow, then read on—this chapter is SO for you!

Welcome back and congratulations *Mrs.* whatever your new last name is! How was the wedding? Fabulous I'm sure! And you were oh so a Zen Bride, right? I'm so proud! And . . .

Now what? Hmmmm, this is the million dollar question. So you've spent all this time completely immersed in planning your wedding—the details, the logistics, the outcome, the ups, the downs, the joy, the love, the chaos, the family drama, the hiccups, the dress, the ceremony, the dancing, the toasts, the food, the cake, the *marriage.*

I remember vaguely hearing during my wedding planning that women tend to go through a "postpartum wedding depression" when it was all done but I truly thought that was preposterous! Ridiculous!

Until I planned my own wedding, got married, honey-mooned, and came back to real life. Then I felt a bit "empty." That certainly was a new (and scary) feeling, after a year of constant chaos.

I think when we're all planning out our weddings, there's a part of us living in a very potent, intense, and passionate world we otherwise only dabble in for many different reasons. But we do live and breathe in this "heightened" state of creativity and passion almost full time when planning our wedding. So what happens then when the stage disappears and all we're left with is what's in front of us? I don't mean to minimize the wedding but let's face it—the wedding is usually a multiple hour event that signals the beginning of a new life. The challenge is that we've spent a year (give or take some months) planning for that 4 hour (read: *hourly*) event instead of planning for the rest of our lives. It's like being in the middle of the most fantastic party and then having to come back the next day and see the club in the normal hours of daylight . . . what does it look like in normal light?

I don't have any "zen" answers to this question (shocking I know!). But I do think it's important to know—*to remember* what you're passionate about in life (remove wedding planning / wedding from the equation)—what brings you joy? It's really this simple. So often we go looking for the most complicated solution or answer. In this case—it's the most simple and obvious . . .

When you're back from the wedding and honeymoon—this is when you will truly realize how much energy and space your wedding planning took—because all of a sudden there will be this unexplainable emptiness (stillness?). This is not a bad thing! It's only when there is empty space that something new can move in (this is my Feng Shui wisdom kicking in) . . . know that now. The question then is: *What brings you joy?!?* And the answer is to figure it out and then, **to do it!**

Take that Thai cooking class you've always wanted to . . . sign up for tango classes with your new hubby . . . join a book club since you love to read . . . the zen solution for being a Zen Bride/Wife is to recognize what is in front of you right now and choose what brings you joy! This is now the most exciting part of it all—your wedding was just the party to get it started . . .

"THE AIM OF LIFE IS TO LIVE,

AND TO LIVE MEANS TO BE AWARE,

JOYOUSLY, DRUNKENLY,

SERENELY, DIVINELY AWARE."

—HENRY MILLER

Journal

"This day I will marry my friend, the one I laugh with, live for, dream with, love."

—ANONYMOUS

"We sat side by side in the morning light and looked out at the future together."

—BRIAN ANDRES

"They gave each other a smile with a future in it."

—RING LARDNER

"Married couples who love each other tell
a thousand things without talking."

—CHINESE PROVERB

"Trip over love, you can get up. Fall in love and you fall forever."

—Unknown

"A successful marriage requires falling in love many times, always with the same person."

—MIGNON MCLAUGHLIN

"All you need is love."

—JOHN LENNON

"Love does not consist of gazing at each other, but in looking together in the same direction."

—ANTOINE DE SAINT-EXUPERY

"To love someone deeply gives you strength. Being loved by someone deeply gives you courage."

—LAO TZU

"Love is, above all, the gift of oneself."

—JEAN ANOUILH

_____

_____

_____

_____

_____

_____

_____

_____

_____

_____

_____

_____

_____

_____

_____

_____

_____

_____

_____

_____

"Take spring when it comes and rejoice.
Take happiness when it comes and rejoice.
Take love when it comes and rejoice."

—CARL EWALD

"You are to me an object intensely desirable—the air
I breathe in a room empty of you is unhealthy."

—JOHN KEATS

"Marriage is a partnership in which each inspire the other, and brings fruition to both of you."

—MILLICENT CAREY MCINTOSH

"Love is a symbol of eternity. It wipes out all sense of time, destroying all memory of a beginning and all fear of an end."

—UNKNOWN